Challenging Math Riddles for Kids

CHALLENGING MATH RIDDLES FOR KIDS

Fun Brainteasers & Logic Games to Develop Math Skills

PATRICIA BARNES

Illustrations by Gareth Williams

ROCKRIDGE
PRESS

Pandora's Box + Mount Browne = Infinity

For general information on our other products and services or to obtain technical support, please contact our Customer Care Department within the United States at (866) 744-2665, or outside the United States at (510) 253-0500.

Rockridge Press publishes its books in a variety of electronic and print formats. Some content that appears in print may not be available in electronic books, and vice versa.

Interior and Cover Designer: Stephanie Mautone
Art Producer: Melissa Malinowksy
Editor: Maxine Marshall
Production Editor: Matthew Burnett
Production Manager: Eric Pier-Hocking

Illustrations © 2021 Gareth Williams

Paperback ISBN: 978-1-63807-387-1
eBook ISBN: 978-1-63878-950-5
R0

contents

Riddle Me This

To solve the riddles in this book, you won't need a pencil and paper, a ruler, or other tools. All you need is this book and your brain—and maybe a few other brains if you want to share these riddles with family or friends! After all, riddles are fun to work on by yourself, but they are even more fun when you have other people around to help puzzle them out.

The riddles in this book are all challenging. They begin at Level 1: Smarty-Pants. The Smarty-Pants riddles are the simplest to solve, but that doesn't mean they are easy! Smarty-Pants riddles show that not everything is as straightforward as it looks.

Level 2 is Brainiac, where the riddles start to get trickier. This might be because the numbers are bigger or perhaps the riddles are more difficult. Level 3 is Genius, and that's where the hardest riddles in the book live.

Each level has a mixture of riddles, some short and some long, plus a few math jokes and a famous math riddle. These classic math riddles from history come with interesting facts about the question plus details about the answer.

Speaking of answers, you can find answers to all of the riddles at the back of the book. Now let's get riddling!

WARM-UP RIDDLES

Riddles are questions that challenge you to think in different ways. To solve some riddles, you have to think hard about what the words mean or discover funny plays on words. Other riddles make you think the question is asking one thing when really it is asking something else.

There are three different types of riddles in this book:

ENIGMAS are riddles that use words to describe something and you have to figure out what is being described. For example:

I have a head and a tail, but I don't have a body. What am I?

HINT: Pick out the important words. This can help you answer a riddle. In this case, the important words are "head" and "tail." What can the words "head" and "tail" refer to, other than parts of a body?

ANSWER: A coin.

CONUNDRUMS are riddles in which one or two words can mean different things. Here's an example:

What is black and white and red all over?

HINT: Look for a word that can be spelled differently or that can have more than one meaning.

ANSWER: A newspaper is black and white and *read* all over.

LATERAL THINKING RIDDLES ask you to think creatively. Sometimes they include extra details to send your thinking in the wrong direction. Try this one:

If an electric train is traveling east at 60 miles per hour and the wind is blowing west at 75 miles per hour, which direction does the train's smoke blow?

HINT: Pick out all of the details and see if they match each other. There might be some extra details included to throw you off.

ANSWER: An electric train doesn't make smoke.

LEVEL 1
SMARTY-PANTS

1. Ash is the 50th fastest runner at school and the 50th slowest runner. How many runners are at Ash's school?

2. A child has a 30-inch-long strip of paper. If they cut off one inch every second, how many seconds does it take to get 30 pieces?

3. Divide 30 by ½ and add 10. What's the answer?

4. Where can you add nine to seven and get four as the correct answer?

5. There are seven games in a box. If you take two games and your friend takes three games, how many games do you have?

6. The butcher is six feet tall, has a 34-inch waist, and wears size-nine shoes. What does the butcher weigh?

7. At the shoe store, they can fit 28 shoes into one case. How many cases will they need for 112 pairs?

8. How are the numbers 8 and 11 similar?

9. Jessie throws a ball onto the roof. The roof is 12 feet off the ground. Jessie takes a ladder, climbs onto the roof, and gets the ball. On the way back down, Jessie falls off the 15-foot-tall ladder but isn't hurt. How?

10. Merrill puts 1 pound of gummy bears on one end of a seesaw and 16 ounces of popcorn on the other. Which end of the seesaw has more weight?

11. A soccer fan knows that the score will be 0–0 before the game. How?

12. Which is written correctly: "8 and 6 ARE 15" or "8 and 6 IS 15"?

13. In Raya's family, there are seven siblings, all born two years apart. If the youngest sibling is seven, how old is the oldest?

14. I have two coins that total 55 cents. One is not a nickel. What coins do I have?

15. A cowboy rode into town on Friday. He slept for 16 hours, danced for 7, played cards for 15, and left on Friday. How?

16. How big will a 45-degree angle be under a microscope that magnifies 10X? What about a microscope that magnifies 15X?

17. Taylor draws a line on a piece of paper. Without changing the line, Taylor makes it longer. How?

18. Why are 2022 dollar bills worth more than 2002 dollar bills?

19. What is the next number in this series?
7,645 . . . 5,764 . . . 4,576 . . .

20. A naughty toddler tears pages 7, 8, 18, 32, and 64 out of a book. How many pages did the toddler tear out?

21. What can you take away from seven to make it even?

22. How much dirt is there in a rectangular hole that is 1 foot deep, 3 feet long, and 5 feet wide?

23. You are in a race with seven other people, and the race is three laps around the track. On the first lap, you are in fourth place. On the second lap, you are in third place. On the last lap, you pass the person in second place. Where do you finish?

24. An alien species uses rocks with numbers written on them as money. If a rock with "one" written on it is worth $3, a rock with "four" written on it is worth $4, and a rock with "three" written on it is worth $5, what's a rock with "seven" written on it worth?

25. What is the next number in the sequence: 2, 4, 8, 10, 20 . . . ?

26. Pick a number. Double it, then multiply it by 4, and then divide it by 8. What do you get?

27. A horse is tied to a 12-foot-long rope. The horse's food is 20 feet away. How does the horse get to the food?

28. What can you put between five and six so the result is bigger than five but less than six?

29. On another planet, 1 = 5, 2 = 10, 3 = 14, and 4 = 20. What does 5 equal?

30. Add one letter to 908 so that it equals 720. What letter did you add?

31. There are 10 flies on the table where you are eating. You use a book to swat three flies. How many are left on the table?

32. A year has 365 days. How many days are in four years?

33. What is half of two plus two?

34. At the movie theater, a popcorn and soda cost $15.10. If the popcorn costs $5 more than the soda, how much does each item cost?

35. What do you get if you multiply all the numbers on a telephone keypad together?

36. If one child takes 90 minutes to clean their room, how long will it take two children to clean the same room?

37. Mo flips a coin eight times. Each time, the coin lands heads up. It is not a trick coin. If Mo flips the coin again, what are the odds it will land tails up?

38. Two trains are on one track. One travels east at 50 mph; one travels west at 100 mph. They cannot slow down or move to another track. If they are 100 miles apart, how long before they crash?

39. How many times can you subtract 5 from 25?

40. You go to the movies and pay for everyone's tickets. Is it cheaper to take two friends once or one friend twice?

41. How can you add eight 8s to total 1,000?

42. The weight of a brick equals 1 pound plus half a brick. How heavy is one brick?

43. You are standing in line before school, and you are currently 10 feet away from the school building. With each step forward, you cover half the distance. How many steps does it take to get there?

44. I live at home with my mother and all my siblings. My mother has three daughters. Each daughter has one brother. I am one brother. How many people live in our house?

45. How many 8s are there between 1 and 100?

46. Al has 20 books on a shelf and numbers them 1 to 20. Al takes 4 to read. How many are left?

47. If the pet shop sells puppies for $40, kittens for $40, and tarantulas for $80, how much is a cockatoo?

48. What's the difference between three dollars and sixty five-cents?

49. What is the next number in this list: 2, 3, 5, 9, 17 . . . ?

50. If you are 10 years old today, and you have a brother half your age, how old will your brother be when you are 14?

51. A year has 12 months, 52 weeks, or 365 days (ignoring leap years, which have an extra day). How many seconds are in a year?

52. At midnight, it's pouring rain. The forecast says it will rain for 18 hours, be dry for 10 hours, rain for 10 hours, and then be dry for 10 hours. Will it be sunny in 48 hours?

53. Cam has a big family with 10 aunts, 10 uncles, and 30 cousins. All of Cam's cousins share an aunt except for Cam. How?

54. If 2 + 2 = 44, 3 + 3 = 96, 4 + 4 = 168, and 5 + 5 = 2510, what does 6 + 6 equal?

55. Candy bars are on sale for $12 a dozen. How many candy bars can you get for $50?

56. Each day, a zoo spends $60 feeding a lion, $80 feeding a tiger, and $110 feeding a leopard. What does the jaguar cost to feed?

57. Can you solve this sum (ignoring order of operations)? 2 + 2 + 2 x 2 + 2 + 2 x 0 + 2 = ?

58. Bee and Boo each start with the same number of nuts. How many nuts does Bee give to Boo so Boo has 10 more nuts than Bee?

59. Can you work out what number comes next in this list? 3, 3, 4, 3, 4, 6, 5, 4, 2, 4 . . .

60. A farmer has 120 sheep. Someone leaves the gate open and all but 47 run away. How many sheep does the farmer have left?

The Sumerian Riddle—the First Riddle in the World

There is a house. One enters it blind and comes out seeing. What is it?

DID YOU KNOW? The riddle implies that before you start studying at school, there are lots of things you do not "see" because you haven't learned them yet. So you are "blind." Then, when you have learned things and come out of school, you know, or "see," more things.

This riddle and its answer were written on a 5,000-year-old stone tablet that archaeologists discovered in the 1800s. There are 25 riddles on the tablet, and scientists think they are the oldest written riddles. When the tablet was discovered, archaeologists could not read the writing. By 1960, people had worked out how to read the tablet, and they discovered a long riddle and an answer. This is a short version of the riddle because nobody has figured out how to translate the rest of the riddle.

ANSWER: A school.

LEVEL 2

BRAINIAC

61. Rohan has a bookshelf in his bedroom. His favorite book is 4th from the left and 6th from the right. How many books are on the shelf?

62. If 1 + 9 + 8 = 1, what does 2 + 8 + 9 equal?

63. A basket holds five apples. How can you give an apple to each of five children and leave one apple in the basket?

64. Three hens lay three eggs in three minutes. If they continue laying at the same speed, how many eggs can they lay in an hour?

65. How can you take 1 away from 29 and be left with 30?

66. With one line, change 101010 to say the time is 9:50.

67. I have 6⅚ piles of sand to my left and 3⅞ on my right. If I put them together, how many sand piles do I have?

68. If you have two twins, three triplets, and four quadruplets, how many people do you have?

69. I have a flashlight that needs 2 batteries. In a drawer, I find 8 batteries, but only 4 of them work. What's the fewest number of pairs I need to test to guarantee I have 2 batteries that work?

70. Two moms and two daughters go into a candy shop together. Both moms and both daughters buy one candy bar each. Candy bars are 50 cents each, and together the moms and daughters spend $1.50. How?

71. Sonali just won the lottery! She has two options for collecting her winnings. Which option will give her more money: (1) collecting a million dollars today or 2) collecting a penny today, two pennies tomorrow, four pennies on day three, and so on, doubling the pennies she receives every day for 31 days?

JOKE

What do you call friends who love math?

ANSWER: AlgeBROS.

72. If 2 = 8, 3 = 27, 4 = 64, and 6 = 216, what does 9 equal?

73. Every year on their birthday, a child visits the amusement park. They were 12 on their last visit and will be 14 on their next visit. How?

74. It takes 10 minutes to fry one grilled cheese sandwich, frying each side for 5 minutes. Two sandwiches fit in a pan. What's the shortest time to fry three sandwiches?

75. A chicken egg takes 3 minutes to boil, a duck egg 5 minutes, and a goose egg 7 minutes. How long does it take to boil all three?

76. Using the numbers 1, 2, 4, 5, 6, and 8 and the symbols (x) and (=), write a correct equation.

77. What's unique about the number 8549176320?

78. If 1 + 1 = 2, 2 + 2 = 8, 3 + 3 = 18, what does 4 + 4 = ?

79. If Mo is 36 inches plus half their height, how tall is Mo?

80. Add mathematical signs (+, −, x, or /, for example) between the numbers to make this equation true: 0123456789 = 1

81. If I am paid $2 for 4, $4 for 40, $6 for 10 and 2, and $8 for 12 and 10, what am I selling, and how much are 10, 12, and 6?

82. If 7 + 7 = 12, 5 + 5 = 8, 3 + 3 = 4, and 2 + 2 = 2, what does 6 + 6 = ?

83. A ship at the dock has a lifeboat hanging off its side. The lifeboat is 15 feet above the water. If the tide rises at a rate of 3½ feet per hour, how long will it take for the water to reach the lifeboat?

84. One airplane is flying from New York to London at 600 mph. Another is flying from London to New York at 500 mph. When the planes meet, which one will be closer to London?

85. How many times a day do the minute hand and the hour hand overlap on a clock?

86. Yellow marbles are 19 millimeters wide. Green marbles are 21 millimeters wide. How many marbles of each color will exactly fill a tube that is 562 millimeters long?

87. You are cleaning your room in the dark. All your socks are on the floor: 30 white socks, 22 black socks, and 14 blue socks. If you are trying to pair the socks by color, what is the minimum number of socks you'd need to pick up to find a matching pair?

88. In question 87, what's the highest number of socks you need to pick up to guarantee you had a blue pair?

89. From which number can you take away half and leave nothing?

90. A babysitter gives a child 12 candies and says they can eat one every half hour. How long will the candies last?

91. What can you do to this equation to make it true?
    81 x 9 = 801

92. How can you add eight 4s together so that the total adds up to 500?

93. Nathan has math class four times a week. If he has math at 8:00 Monday, 9:20 on Tuesday, 10:40 on Wednesday, and 1:20 on Friday, what time is math on Thursday?

94. Ali died 135 years after Amir was born. At the time of each of their deaths, their combined age was 110 years. If Ali died in the year 57 BCE, in what year was Amir born?

95. If there are three cups of sugar and you take one away, how many do you have?

96. 57 pennies fit in one cup, and a piggy bank can hold 3 ½ cups. How many pennies can fit in an empty piggy bank?

97. A clothing store owner has made up their own system for deciding the price of items. A jacket costs $30, socks cost $25, a hat is $15, and a shirt is $25. Using the shopkeeper's secret method, how much does underwear cost?

98. Taylor has 87 chickens that together lay 261 eggs per week. Taylor wants more eggs to sell at the market and increases the flock by adding 45 percent more roosters. How many eggs will Taylor have each week now?

99. What do you get if you add 2 to 200 four times?

100. What number comes next in this sequence?
1, 4, 7, 11, 15, 19 . . .

101. How long will a 12-inch ruler be when you look at it through a microscope that magnifies objects 10 times?

102. If a clock chimes six times in five minutes, how many times will it chime in 10 minutes?

103. Jess wants 250 ribbons, each 3½ inches long. The ribbons are sold in 6-foot-long spools. How many spools will Jess need?

104. How would you arrange 2, 3, 4, 5, and the symbols "+" and "=" to make a correct equation?

105. How do you make the equation 1 + 9 + 1 = 150 true by adding one line?

106. Fifty minutes ago, it was four times as many minutes past 7 p.m. as the number of minutes it currently is until 10 p.m. What time is it?

107. A child dropped a book in the library and it made a loud bang, causing everyone to turn and look. Twenty eyes were on the child. How many people were in the library?

108. After a heavy snowfall, Jeff's garden has twice as much snow as their next-door neighbor's. Why? (Nothing is preventing the snow from falling on either garden.)

109. How can you write twenty and add one so it becomes nineteen?

110. What letter comes next? 1, 2, 3 (s), 4, 5, 6 (f), 7, 7, 1 (f), 3, 9, 7 . . .

111. You're taking homemade brownies to a friend's house. On the way, you cross five bridges. At each bridge, you must pay a toll of half your brownies. Each toll-taker will give you back one brownie. How many brownies do you need to start with to end up with 2 for your friend?

112. There are three bridges on a road, and each has a guard. To get past the guard, you must answer their question correctly. The first guard asks, "Six?" and you answer three. The guard lets you pass. The second guard asks, "Twelve?" and you answer six. Again, the guard lets you pass. When the next guard asks, "Ten?" you answer five, but they don't let you pass. Why?

113. I have four rolls of cloth, each 100 feet long. I have a machine that cuts the fabric into 1-foot lengths, making one cut every 4 seconds. Ignoring any time for swapping the rolls, how long will it take for the machine to cut all four rolls into 100 pieces each?

114. If six thousand, six hundred, and six dollars is written as $6,606, write eleven thousand, eleven hundred, and eleven dollars.

115. What number is missing from this series? 16, 06, 68, 88, X, 98

116. Can you arrange four nines in an equation to equal 100?

117. Walking to school, you count 20 houses on your right. Walking home, you count 20 on your left. How many houses did you pass on your walk?

118. The day before yesterday, Alex was 17. Next year Alex will be 20. What day is Alex's birthday?

119. How many 6 inch x 2 inch bricks does it take to complete a 30 foot x 30 foot x 20 foot brick building?

120. A landscaper must plant four trees so that each one is precisely the same distance from the other trees. How do they do this?

The Life of Diophantus

Diophantus was a kid for ⅙ of his life. He grew his first beard in the next 1/12 of his life. At the end of the next 1/7 of his life, Diophantus got married. Five years after he got married, his son was born. His son was in Greece for ½ of Diophantus's life. Diophantus left Greece four years after his son left Greece. How long did Diophantus live?

DID YOU KNOW? We don't know very much about the ancient Greek mathematician Diophantus. A lot of what we do know comes from this riddle, written by one of his fans. The riddle is written as an algebraic equation because Diophantus is known as the "father of algebra."

LEVEL 3

GENIUS

121.   When does 50 + 50 = 75?

122.   You have two ropes. Each rope takes exactly 1 hour to burn completely. How can you burn the two ropes in a total of 45 minutes without cutting them?

123.   If Susan receives a score of 10, Arabella receives 20, and Jim receives 5, by the same system, what score does Jennifer receive?

124.   A frog is stuck at the bottom of a 20-foot hole. How many jumps does it take to escape if it jumps up 5 feet and then falls back 4 feet?

125. In 1990, Erin was 15 years old. In 1995, Erin was 10 years old. How?

126. What's ½ of ⅔ of ¾ of ⅘ of ⅚ of ⁶⁄₇ of ⅞ of ⁸⁄₉ of ⁹⁄₁₀ of 10,000?

127. If 1203 = 1, 4566 = 2, 8898 = 7, 4566 = 2, 5464 = 1, and 7774 = 0, what does 4500 = ?

128. When is 99 more than 100?

129. Train tickets are 50 cents each. A rider goes to the ticket booth and hands the cashier $1.00. The cashier hands the rider two tickets. How did the cashier know to give the rider two tickets instead of one ticket and change if neither of them spoke?

130. Jezz finds five gold chains, and wants to make them into one long necklace. Each chain has six links. The jeweler charges $10 for every link they have to open and reclose. What is the least amount of money that Jezz can spend to make a necklace that uses links from all five chains?

131. If you're born in an odd-numbered year (like 2009), will you celebrate your 30th birthday in an odd year or an even one? Don't forget leap years!

132. If 4 + 2 = 26, 8 + 1 = 79, and 6 + 5 = 111 what does 7 + 3 = ?

133. Hanna and her father are growing tomatoes in their garden. A tomato grows every 5¼ inches on a vine. If the vine is 9.2 feet long, how many vegetables can they expect to grow?

134. You have 1,000 small cubes stacked to make a large 10 x 10 x 10 cube. If you take off one layer of cubes, how many are left?

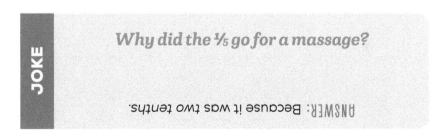

135. Ash hammers a nail into a tree to mark his height. If the tree grows 15 inches a year, how much higher is the nail in 67 months?

136. A candy store is hosting a recycling drive. Customers can exchange four candy bar wrappers for one new candy bar. How many bars can you get with 64 wrappers?

137. A chessboard is an 8 x 8 grid of alternating black and white tiles. How many squares are on a chessboard?

138. The hot faucet takes 15 minutes to fill the bath, and the cold faucet takes 12 minutes. The bath empties in 10 minutes. If you forget to put in the plug but run both the hot and cold faucets, how long does it take to fill the bath?

139. Nine balls look the same, but one is slightly heavier than the others. How can you find the heaviest ball using a balance scale just twice?

140. In a bicycle race, the rider who finished two places in front of the last rider finishes one ahead of the rider who comes in fifth. How many people were in the race?

141. If 125 + 0 = 18, 236 + 0 = 26, and 347 + 0 = 34, what does 458 + 0 = ?

142. Sam was born on January 1, 23 BCE, and died on January 2, 23 CE. How old was Sam when they died?

143. Every morning, Drew drives to the train station at an average speed of 30 mph, arriving just in time to catch the train. This morning, there was a car accident at the halfway point of Drew's commute, which caused traffic to slow down. While stuck in traffic, Drew looks down and discovers their average speed, so far, has only been 14 mph. In order to catch the train, what average speed does Drew have to drive for the rest of the journey?

144. Lindsay's friends want to buy her a surprise birthday gift that costs X dollars. Each friend will give the same amount of money toward the gift. Ten friends offer to give money, but then two people drop out. The eight remaining friends provide an extra dollar each, so they have enough. How much is the gift?

145. Move one digit to make this equation correct:
$101 - 102 = 1$

146. At the bookstore, books are on sale at 20 percent off the original price. By what percentage of the sale price do you have to increase the cost to sell them at the original price again?

147. Which triangle has a larger perimeter: one with sides of 3, 4, and 5 inches or one with sides of 3, 4, and 7 inches?

148. Outside the school window, Shae sees a flock of ducks. There are two ducks in front of two other ducks, two ducks behind two other ducks, and two ducks beside two other ducks. How many ducks are there?

149. How long does a 300-foot-long train take to travel through a 300-foot-long tunnel at 300 feet per minute?

150. A farmer builds a square fence with 27 fence poles on each side of the square. How many poles did they use?

151. What's the next number in this sequence?
1, 11, 21, 1211, 111221, 312211 . . .

152. Audrey can pull a loaded wagon 100 feet in
30 seconds. Bradley can pull a wagon of the
same weight half as far in twice the time. How
far in total can both children pull their wagons in
15 seconds?

153. A particular species of plant doubles in size every
day. If it takes 18 days for the plant to cover half
of a lake, how many days will it take two plants to
cover half of the lake?

154. In my top drawer, I have four socks that are either black or white. If I take two socks out of the drawer, the probability that they are a pair of white socks is ½. What's the probability I pull out a black pair?

155. Kali and Lei run a 100-meter race. Kali wins the race, beating Lei by five meters. Kali wants to make things fair when they race again and begins five meters behind the start line. Assuming that they both run at the same speed they did in the first race, who will win the second race?

156. Mel measures a plant to chart its growth. At the end of the first month, the plant has increased its height by half. At the end of the second month, it has increased its height by one-third. At the end of the third month, it has increased its height by a quarter, and so on. How many months does it take for the plant to grow 100 times its original height?

157. Sal likes 225 but not 224; 900 but not 800; 144 but not 145. Does Sal like 1600 or 1700?

158. How can you cut a round cake into eight equal slices with three cuts?

159. What is the next number in this sequence? 1, 2, 6, 15, 31 . . .

160. Kit has some bendable metal wires and wants to make a cube. What's the minimum number of wires Kit needs, and how many joins must they glue together?

161. What are the next four numbers in this series? 11, 15, 19, 18, 26, 21, 32 . . .

162. Jack, Vee, and Zara are at the park. Jack has 36 candies, Vee has 45 candies, and Zara has 9 dimes. The three share the candies equally, and Zara gives Jack and Vee the 90 cents. How do Jack and Vee divide the money according to the pieces of candy they each gave Zara?

163. You drive with your dad to the ice cream store going 20 mph. On the way home, your dad takes the same route going 30 mph. Not counting the time spent at the ice cream store, what was your dad's average speed?

164. If 2 + 3 = 8, 4 + 5 = 24, 6 + 7 = 42, and 8 + 9 = 80, what does 9 + 10 = ?

165. Mrs. Maple has two children. Her older child is a girl. What is the probability that Mrs. Maple has two daughters?

166. At six o'clock, the clock chimes six times. There are 30 seconds between the first and last chimes. At 12 o'clock, how many seconds will pass between the first and last chimes?

167. A child has flipped two coins. If at least one of the coins has landed heads up and the probability of any coin landing heads up is $^5/_{50}$, what are the chances the other coin lands tails up?

168. If 63AC = FC19 and 91AG = IA2549, what does 85DM = ?

169. Val has a 100-pound watermelon and leaves it lying out in the sun. Ninety-nine percent of the watermelon's weight is water. After the watermelon has been in the sun for a few hours, 98 percent of its weight is water. How much water has evaporated?

170. Yoshie buys two phones and then sells them to friends for $600 each. Yoshie takes a loss of 20 percent on one and makes a profit of 20 percent on the other. How much did the phones cost, and did Yoshie make a profit or lose money overall?

171. What numbers are angry?

172. You drop 100 coins in the dark. Ninety coins fall heads up, and 10 coins fall tails up. Still in the dark, can you sort the coins into two piles so there are the same number of tails-up coins in each pile when the lights go on?

173. If a special holiday occurs only on the first day of a new century, what are the chances that the holiday will be on a Sunday?

174. Evey is moving, leaving behind 51 books. Evey tells James they can have half of the books, Josh can have one-third, and Gabe can have one-ninth. The three can't work out how to do this, but Evey helps them out. How does Evey solve the problem?

175. What are the missing numbers in this sequence?
31, 62, X, 25, 56, X, 19, 401, X

The Fork in the Road

You come to a fork in the road and don't know which way is safest. Each fork has a guard, one who always lies and the other who always tells the truth. You don't know which guard is which. What do you ask to find the road you want?

DID YOU KNOW? Ask this question, and one guard will tell the truth about a lie, while the other will tell a lie about the truth. So any answer either guard gives is always the opposite of the correct answer.

A version of this riddle is in the children's movie *Labyrinth*. Sarah has to rescue her baby brother from an evil goblin king, making her way through a maze, solving riddles and puzzles on the way. At one point, she meets two guards who ask her this riddle.

ANSWER: You ask: "Would the other guard tell me that your path is the one I want?"

ANSWER KEY

LEVEL 1: SMARTY-PANTS

1. 99 runners. There are 49 runners faster than Ash and 49 who are slower.

2. 29 seconds because the 29th cut makes two pieces.

3. 70. 30 divided by half is 60, not 15. Add 10 and you get 70.

4. A clock. At nine o'clock, add seven hours, and it is four o'clock.

5. Two. You took two games from the box, so you have two games.

6. Meat! The question asks what the butcher weighs, not the butcher's weight.

7. Eight cases. Each case can hold 28 shoes or 14 pairs.

8. Both are the same number flipped upside down.

9. Jesse falls from the bottom rung of the ladder.

10. One pound is 16 ounces. Both ends of the seesaw have equal weight.

11. The score is always 0–0 before the game.

12. Neither, because 8 + 6 = 14.

13. 19. The siblings are 7, 9, 11, 13, 15, 17, and 19.

14. A 50-cent coin and a nickel.

15. Friday is the name of the cowboy's horse.

16. It will always be 45 degrees. The degree of the angle does not change under magnification.

17. Taylor draws a shorter line next to the first line. Now the first line is longer.

18. Because there are more of them. 2022 and 2002 are the numbers of dollar bills, not the year they were made.

19. 6,457. The last digit is moved from the end of the number to the beginning.

20. Four. Pages 7 and 8 are two sides of the same page.

21. S. Seven – S = even.

22. There's zero dirt in the hole. If there were dirt, it wouldn't be a hole.

23. Second place. When you pass the person in second place, you take their position, and they drop to third.

24. $5. Each letter is worth $1, and "seven" has five letters.

25. 22. Each number alternates between +2 and x2. So 2; (+2 =) 4; (x2 =) 8; (+2 =); 10 (x2 =); 20 (+2=) 22.

26. The number you started with. Doubling a number and multiplying it by four is canceled out when you divide the number by eight.

27. The horse walks over because the other end of the rope isn't tied to anything.

28. A decimal point, making the number 5.6.

29. 1. The beginning of the question says 1 = 5.

30. Add an X between 90 and 8: 90 x 8 = 720.

31. The three flies you swatted. The other flies will fly away.

32. 1,461. One of the years is a leap year with an extra day, so (365 x 4) + 1 = 1,461.

33. Three. Half of two is one, plus two equals three.

34. The popcorn costs $10.05, and the soda costs $5.05.

35. 0. Any number multiplied by zero equals zero.

36. No time. The children wouldn't have to clean the same room; it is already clean.

37. $5/50$. The odds are $5/50$ every time you flip a coin.

38. They don't crash. They are traveling away from each other.

39. Once. When you subtract 5 from 25, it becomes 20, so you can't subtract 5 from 25 again.

40. Two friends once, which requires three tickets. If you take one friend twice, you're buying four tickets (two for you and two for your friend).

41. 888 + 88 + 8 + 8 + 8 = 1,000.

42. 2 pounds. Half a brick is 1 pound, plus 1 pound = 2 pounds.

43. You never get there. Each step can only take you half the distance.

44. Five people including the mother. Each sister has one brother, not one brother each.

45. 19. 8, 18, 28, 38, 48, 58, 68, 78, 80, 81, 82, 83, 84, 85, 86, 87, 88, 89, and 98.

46. 19. Al takes book number 4, not 4 books.

47. $20. Animals cost $10 per leg.

48. Nothing. Sixty five-cent coins equal $3.

49. 33. Double the previous number and subtract 1.

50. 9. Your brother is half your age now, so he is 5. When you're 14, your brother will also be 4 years older.

51. 12. January second, February second, March second, and so on.

52. No, because in 48 hours it will be midnight.

53. Their aunt is Cam's mother.

54. 3612. The first part of each answer is the two digits multiplied, in this case, 6 and 6. The second part is the two digits added. 6 x 6 = 36 and 6 + 6 = 12.

55. 50. The candy bars are $1 each.

56. $90. Each day, they spend $20 per consonant and $10 per vowel in the name of the animal. "Jaguar" has 3 consonants and 3 vowels.

57. 2, because everything before the last 2 is multiplied by 0.

58. Five. Imagine they have 100 nuts each. Bee gives 5 nuts to Boo, keeping 95 for herself. Now Boo has 105, 10 more than Bee.

59. 4. Each digit is the number of letters in each word of the question.

60. 47. All *but* 47 ran away, so the farmer is left with 47 sheep.

LEVEL 2: BRAINIAC

61. Nine, including his favorite book. There are three books to the left of his favorite book and five to the right.

62. 10. The result is the initial letters of the numbers in each equation. **O**ne + **N**ine + **E**ight = **ONE** and **T**wo + **E**ight + **N**ine = **TEN**.

63. You give one apple each to four children and give the fifth child the basket containing the last apple.

64. 60. The three hens lay one egg per minute between them.

65. With Roman numerals, 29 is XXIX. Take away I leaving XXX, which is 30.

66. 10**T**010 or Ten "To" Ten.

67. One. Put them together, and you have one big pile of sand.

68. Nine. The question didn't say two *sets* of twins, triplets, and quadruplets.

69. 6 pairs of batteries. Split the batteries into two groups of three and one group of two. This guarantees you have two working batteries in at least one group. The worst-case scenario is that each group of three has only one good battery so none of the pairings work. So you know the group of two is good and you don't have to test them.

70. A child, a mom, and a grandmother. The mom is both a mom and a daughter.

71. Option 2. At the end of 31 days, Sonali will have 1,073,741,823 pennies or $10,737,418.23.

72. 729. Each number is multiplied by a power of 3. So 9 x 9 x 9 = 729.

73. Today is their 13th birthday.

74. 15 minutes. Put sandwiches A and B into the pan. After five minutes, flip sandwich A, take sandwich B out of the pan, and put sandwich C in. After another five minutes, take sandwich A out, ▶

flip sandwich C, and put sandwich B back in to fry the other side. Sandwiches B and C will be done five minutes later.

75. Seven minutes. Put them all in the same pot, take the chicken egg out after 3 minutes, the duck egg out after 5 minutes, and the goose egg out after 7 minutes.

76. There are two answers: 64 x 8 = 512 and 52 x 8 = 416. Nothing in the question says you have to use the numbers in the order given.

77. It is the only number that uses every digit arranged in alphabetical order.

78. 32. Multiply the numbers in the equation and then double the answer. 4 x 4 = 16, doubled is 32.

79. 72 inches. Half of Mo's height is 36 inches, so their full height is double that.

80. 0 + 1 + 2 + 3 + 4 – 5 + 6 + 7 – 8 – 9 = 1.

81. The candles cost $2 each, so 10 + 12 + 6 will be $10.

82. 10. Subtract one from both numbers in each equation and add them.

83. The entire ship will rise with the tide, so the distance between the water and the lifeboat will remain the same.

84. When they meet, they are both in the same place, so they will both be the same distance from London.

85. 22 times: 12:00:00, 1:05:27, 2:10:55, 3:16:22, 4:21:49, 5:27:16, 6:32:44, 7:38:11, 8:43:38, 9:49:05, 10:54:33. Each twice a day.

86. 13 yellow and 15 green marbles. 13 x 19 = 247, 15 x 21 = 315, 247 + 315 = 562.

87. Four socks. Even if each of your first three socks were a different color, the fourth has to make a pair.

88. 54. It's possible to pick up all the white socks (30) and all the black socks (22) before picking up two blue socks. 30 + 22 + 2 = 54.

89. Eight. If you take away the top half of a written eight, you are left with the bottom half, which looks like a zero.

90. 5½ hours. The child eats the first candy at 0 hours, the second at 30 minutes, the third at 1 hour, and so on.

91. Flip it upside down. 108 = 6 x 18.

92. 444 + 44 + 4 + 4 + 4 = 500.

93. Nathan doesn't have math class on Thursday.

94. 32 BCE. If Ali died 135 years after Amir was born and their combined age when they died was 110, there must have been 25 years when neither of them was alive. So Ali must have been born in 32 BCE—20 years after Amir died.

95. One. You took away one cup of sugar.

96. One. Once you put a penny in the piggy bank, it is no longer empty.

97. $45. The shopkeeper charges $5 per letter in the name of the item.

98. 261. Roosters don't lay eggs.

99. 202, 202, 202, and 202.

100. 17. You are looking for the lowest possible number that, when spelled out, contains the number of letters that is next in the sequence. "One" has three letters, "four" has four letters, "seven" has five letters, "eleven" has six letters, ▸

"fifteen" has seven letters, "nineteen" has eight letters, and "seventeen" has nine letters.

101. It will still be the same size. It only looks bigger.

102. 11 times. The first chime is at 0 minutes, the second chime is at 1 minute, and so on.

103. 13. A 6-foot-long spool is 72 inches. 72 divided by 3½ is 20.57, so there's a maximum of 20 3½-inch ribbons per spool. For 250 ribbons, divide 250 by 20 and you get 12½, which you have to round up to 13 spools.

104. 2 + 5 = 3 + 4.

105. Add a line to turn the first plus sign into a 4 to make it 149 + 1 = 150.

106. 9:34 p.m.

107. 11 people. Twenty eyes belonging to 10 people, plus the child.

108. Jeff's garden is twice as big as their neighbor's.

109. XIX. 20 is XX in Roman numerals. XX + I = XIX, or 19.

110. N. Add each group of three numbers and then use the first letter of the answer: 3 + 9 + 7 = 19.

111. Two. At each toll, you pay half of your brownies (one), and the toll-taker gives you back one brownie, so you end up with the same number you started with.

112. Three. The answer is the number of letters in the word the guard asks, not half of the number they provide.

113. 1,584 seconds. Each roll requires 99 cuts to make 100 pieces. One cut every four seconds means 4 x 99=396 seconds per roll. To cut four rolls that each take 396 seconds: 4 x 396 = 1,584 seconds.

114. $12,111. That's 11,000 plus 1,100 plus 11.

115. 87. Turn the page upside down to see 86, X, 88, 89, 90, 91.

116. 99 + 9 / 9 = 100.

117. 20. The houses on your right on the way to school are the same houses on your left on the way home.

118. Alex's birthday is on December 31. Two days ago was December 30, and Alex was 17; Alex's 18th birthday was yesterday, on December 31, which was last year. On December 31 this year, Alex will be 19, and next year he will turn 20.

119. One—the last one.

120. The landscaper plants three of the trees in an equal triangle. He plants the fourth on a hill in the triangle's center.

LEVEL 3: GENIUS

121. When calculating percentages. For example, if an item goes on sale for 50 percent off and you take another 50 percent off of that, the total is 75 percent off.

122. Light one rope at one end and the other rope at both ends. In 30 minutes, the rope you lit at both ends will be burned. Now light both ends of the remaining rope, and it will burn in 15 minutes.

123. 15. The system awards 5 points for each syllable in their name.

124. 16. The frog jumps 5 feet and slides down 4, ending the jump at 1 foot. It then reaches 6 feet but slides back to 2 feet, and so on. On the fifteenth jump, the frog slides back to 15 feet, and on the 16th jump, the frog jumps five feet and is out of the hole.

125. Erin was born in 2005 BCE.

126. 1,000. Multiply all the fractions, and all but ⅒ are canceled out.

127. 2. Count the number of circles in the digits of each figure.

128. On a microwave. Press "99" on a microwave, and it runs for 1 minute and 39 seconds. Press "100" and it runs for 1 minute.

129. The rider gave the cashier four quarters. If the rider only wanted one ticket, they would have handed over two quarters.

130. $40. The jeweler can open four links of one chain and use those links to join the other four chains, creating a necklace of 28 links.

131. An odd year. Leap years don't affect the sequence!

132. 410. Subtract the second number of the equation from the first for the first digit of our answer. Add both numbers in the equation to get the second digit.

133. Zero, because tomatoes are fruits, not vegetables.

134. 512. Take an entire layer off all the way around, and you're left with an 8 x 8 x 8 cube.

135. The nail will be at about the same height because trees grow from the top.

136. 21. After you eat the first 16 bars, you have 16 more wrappers. With these, you can buy four bars. Then you have four wrappers with which to buy one bar.

137. 204 squares: 64 1 x 1 squares, 49 2 x 2, 36 3 x 3, 25 4 x 4, 16 5 x 5, 9 6 x 6, 4 7 x 7, and 1 8 x 8.

138. 20 minutes. In one minute, the hot faucet fills $\frac{1}{15}$ of the bath and the cold fills $\frac{1}{12}$, but $\frac{1}{10}$ of the bath empties: $\frac{1}{15}$ (hot) $+\frac{1}{12}$ (cold) $- \frac{1}{10}$ (empty) $= \frac{3}{60}$ or $\frac{1}{20}$. One-twentieth of the bath fills in one minute, so the bath fills in 20 minutes.

139. Weigh one group of three balls (group A) against another group of three balls (group B). If one side is heavier, you know that group contains the heavy ball. If groups A and B are equal, group C has the heavy ball. Now you have three balls. Take two balls and put one on each side of the scale. If the scale goes down on one side, that side has the heavy ball. If the scale stays balanced, you know the third ball (not on the scale) is the heavy ball.

140. Six. The rider in the question finished fourth.

141. 42. First, add all the numerals in the first number together. For example, 125 becomes $1 + 2 + 5 = 8$. Next, add "number X." In the first equation "number X" is 10. So you have $8 + \mathbf{10} = 18$. Now, here's the tricky part: "number X" increases by five for each equation in the series. So $236 + 0 = 26$ becomes $2 + 3 + 6 = 11$; then $11 + \mathbf{15} = 26$. The next equation is $347 + 0 = 34$, which becomes $3 + 4 + 7 = 14$; then $14 + \mathbf{20} = 34$. Finally, $458 + 0 = 42$ becomes $4 + 5 + 8 = 17$; then $17 + \mathbf{25} = 42$.

142. 45. There's no year zero.

143. Drew can't catch the train because it's already leaving the station.

144. $40. Each of the eight remaining friends gives an extra $1, meaning they were $8 short when the two other friends dropped out, so ▶

the two who dropped out must have been giving $4 each.

145. $101 - 10^2 = 1$.

146. 25 percent. If a $10 book is reduced by 20 percent, the price will drop to $8. To change it back to the original price, we must add $2, which is 25 percent of $8.

147. A triangle with sides of 3, 4, and 5 inches. It's impossible to make a triangle with sides of 3, 4, and 7 inches.

148. Four ducks in a 2 x 2 square.

149. 2 minutes. One minute for the front of the train to clear the tunnel. As it does, the rear is entering the tunnel and clears the tunnel in another minute.

150. 104. One in each corner and 25 between each pair.

151. 13112221. Each number in the sequence describes the number that comes before it. So one is one one, 11 is two ones, and so on.

152. 62.5 feet. Audrey can pull the wagon 100 feet in 30 seconds, which is 200 feet per minute. Bradley can pull their wagon half as far (50 feet) in twice as long (one minute). Fifteen seconds is one-quarter of a minute. In 15 seconds, Audrey can pull their wagon 50 feet, and Bradley can pull theirs 12.5 feet.

153. 17 days. One plant covers ¼ lake in 17 days, so two plants will cover half.

154. Zero. The probability of picking out a pair of white socks is 1 in 2, so there can't be a black pair of socks in the drawer. If there were a black pair, the chance of pulling out a white pair would have been 1 in 3.

155. Kali. Kali runs 100 meters in the time it takes Lei to run 95. When Lei hits the 95-meter mark, Kali will too. Then Kali will pass Lei and win again.

156. 198 months. For example, if the plant were 1 foot tall when Mel begins charting its growth, in month one, it would grow ½ foot. Then in month two, it would grow ⅓ of 1½ feet, which is ½ foot. The plant grows ½ foot every month.

157. 1600. Sal likes perfect squares.

158. Cut the cake in half through the middle, hamburger style. Then from the top cut once across the center of the cake. Finally, cut again across the center perpendicular to the second cut.

159. 56. The sequence takes the first number and adds a perfect square. $1 + 1^2 = 1 + 1 = 2$. Then the answer is added to the next perfect square to get the next number $2 + 2^2 = 2 + 4 = 6$. So $6 + 3^2 = 6 + 9 = 15$, $15 + 4^2 = 15 + 16 = 31$, and $31 + 5^2 = 31 + 25 = 56$.

160. 4 wires, 8 joins

161. The next four numbers are 24, 37, 27, 40. Start by separating out every other number so you have two series. One series is 15, 18, 21, and these numbers increase by three each time, so the next numbers in the series are 24 and 27. The other series is 11, 19, 26, 32, and these numbers increase by one less each time. $11 + 8 = 19$, $19 + 7 = 26$, $26 + 6 = 32$; then $32 + 5 = 37$ and $37 + 4 = 41$.

162. Jack gets 30 cents and Vee gets 60 cents. There were 81 candies altogether, 27 for each child. Jack has 36 candies, keeps 27, and gives his remaining 9 to Zara. Vee has 45 candies, keeps 27, and gives her remaining ▶

18 to Zara. Zara paid for 27 candies with nine dimes. 27 / 9 = 3, so each dime bought 3 candies. Jack gave Zara 9 candies, so he gets 30 cents. Vee gave Zara 18 candies, so she gets 60 cents.

163. 24 mph. Let's say the ice cream store is 60 miles away. It would take three hours at 20 mph to arrive and two hours at 30 mph. That's 120 miles in five hours. 120 / 5 = 24.

164. 99. Multiply the first two numbers in each equation, and then add the first number.

165. One in two. The possibilities are girl/girl or girl/boy.

166. 66 seconds. There are five intervals between strikes when the clock strikes six. Each interval is 6 seconds (30 / 5 = 6). When the clock strikes 12, there will be 11 intervals of 6 seconds each.

167. One in three. You can flip two coins, and they will land in one of these four combinations: heads then heads; heads then tails; tails then tails; or tails then heads. You only know that one coin has landed heads up, so the tails then tails combination is not possible. Because you don't know if the heads-up coin was flipped first or second, any of the other three combinations are possible.

168. HE413. The numbers on the left of the equation are the positions in the alphabet of the letters on the right and vice versa.

169. 50 pounds. In the end, the 1 pound of other stuff is 2 percent, so the total weight is 50 pounds. 50 pounds – 1 pound = 49 pounds water. 99 pounds – 49 pounds = 50 pounds water lost.

170. The phones were $500 and $750. Yoshie sold the pair for $1,200, taking a $50 loss overall.

171. 1, 1000, 51, 6, and 500 in Roman numerals spell "IM LIVID."

172. Make two piles, one with 90 coins and one with 10 coins. Then, flip all the coins in the pile of 10. There are three possible outcomes, all of which would leave you with the same number of tails-up coins in each pile. Scenario 1: You selected all 10 tails-up coins in your pile of 10. Once you flipped them, you would have no tails-up coins in either pile. Scenario 2: Your pile of 10 included no tails-up coins. When you flip them, you would then have 10 tails-up coins in each pile. Scenario 3: You selected a mix of tails-up and heads-up coins for your pile of 10. If you selected X number of tails-up coins, then you would have (10 - X) number of heads. The tails in the original group would be 10 - (10 - X) = X, leaving X number of tails-up coins in both groups.

173. Zero. The first day of a new century never falls on a Sunday, Wednesday, or Friday.

174. Evey adds three books to the 51, making 54. James gets half of 54, which is 27, Josh gets one-third of 54, which is 18, and Gabe gets one-ninth of 54, which is 6. 27 + 18 + 6 = 51 books, leaving Evey to take back the three they added.

175. 93, 87, 721. Each number is the next multiple of 13 in reverse.

ABOUT THE AUTHOR

PATRICIA BARNES has taught almost every age-group, from toddlers to adult learners, and every learning type—from those who have additional struggles in the classroom to those who are cleverer than she can ever hope to be. Having taught in elementary schools, high schools, universities, and corporate boardrooms, Barnes's biggest challenge has been homeschooling her own children. Through homeschooling five kids of varying abilities, some of whom are reluctant students, Barnes has discovered interesting, inspiring, and flexible ways to share her love of learning. She hopes to help others find that same joy.

Printed in the USA
CPSIA information can be obtained
at www.ICGtesting.com
CBHW040741280124
3678CB00006B/52

9 781638 073871